A Cast of Characters

poems by

Teresa McLamb Blackmon

Finishing Line Press
Georgetown, Kentucky

A Cast of Characters

Copyright © 2023 by Teresa McLamb Blackmon
ISBN 979-8-88838-275-2 First Edition
All rights reserved under International and Pan-American Copyright Conventions. No part of this book may be reproduced in any manner whatsoever without written permission from the publisher, except in the case of brief quotations embodied in critical articles and reviews.

ACKNOWLEDGMENTS

"Huck's Heaven" Johnston County Arts Council 2021

Publisher: Leah Huete de Maines

Editor: Christen Kincaid

Cover Art and Design: Mary Humphrey

Author Photo: Ken Tart

Order online: www.finishinglinepress.com
also available on amazon.com

Author inquiries and mail orders:
Finishing Line Press
PO Box 1626
Georgetown, Kentucky 40324
USA

Table of Contents

Henny Penny 1

Unraveled 2

Stupid Poem 3

Measurements 4

The Outcast 5

My Precious One 6

Aylmer's Infomercial 7

All-American 8

Letting Go 9

Wanted 10

Preference 11

Lucrece and the Modern Woman 12

The Ides of March 13

Huck's Heaven 14

Melinoe's Curse 16

Delights 17

The Land that Holds Me 19

In the Harbor 20

Horizons 21

This collection of poems is dedicated to Mamie Lou Johnson, Louise Lambert, Dr. Harry West, Dr. Shelby Stephenson, Dr. Marvin Hester, Dr. Elliot Engel, and Dr. Barbara Baines. Thanks to these teachers I have life-long friends. With great pleasure, I have introduced these literary characters to the many students who sat in my classroom. May they live forever!

"Real people are made out of a whole lot of things—flesh, bones, blood, nerves, and stuff like that. Literary characters are made out of words."
        Thomas C. Foster

"Even after a thousand pages we don't want to leave the world the writer has made for us, or the make-believe people who live there."
        Stephen King

Henny Penny

When I first read Henny Penny,
I worried that the sky would fall,
land on my five-year-old head
and kill me dead.
I figured if Henny Penny could die,
so could I.

Unraveled
(Edgar Lee Masters' "Franklin Jones")

A few hundred Franklin Joneses live in town.
Little brick homes line the streets
like a Monopoly board game.
Manicured lawns map the yards like squares on a quilt.
Sidewalks knit the homes together.
Careful hands guide this tapestry.

Every Franklin hides, afraid of becoming a
slipped stitch, straying from the pattern
before his eyes. He chooses all the right
colors, muted, shaded, pale, mostly.
He shies away from lively colors which would paint
him daring or different.

No one in town chooses his own way, picks
his own fabric, terrified to waver from
the expected. He is lonely and loveless,
but unwilling to open his tightly-shut
blinds. He is bored and without purpose.
He has lost his way.

The meaningless in his life tortures
him into madness and he does nothing,
makes nothing, thinks nothing.
Franklin unravels slowly, the thread of
his life falls to the floor.
The cat paws the leftovers.

Stupid Poem
    (William Carlos Williams' "The Red Wheelbarrow")

Students never understood William Carlos Williams' poem,
"The Red Wheelbarrow." They often exclaimed,
"I could have written that." And I replied, "But you didn't."

"So what's the deal with a red wheelbarrow and wet chickens?"
"Would it matter if the wheelbarrow had not been red?"
"No, it's just a stupid wheelbarrow."

"Have you ever eaten chicken nuggets?"
"Don't be silly. Of course I have."
"And who raised those white chickens?

"I know. Processing plants."
"So processing plants have always existed?
Did you know any farmers?"

"Nope. We don't need them anymore.
We have huge grocery stores now."
"And the shopping carts are wet?"

Measurements
      (T. S. Eliot's "The Love Song of J. Alfred Prufrock")

Prufrock measured life in coffee spoons,
and I have measured too. This morning, at sixty-six,
my years are measured not by spoons
but by something bigger, like a ladle, a muffin
tin, a Pyrex bowl.

Mile posts mark travels down roads framed
with cornfields, old barns, cigarette billboards.
Interstates drag like lazy feet to places so far away.
They try to make a home but fail after a few
days of pretending.

Breath paces my days, and as predictable as sunrise
I measure the hours, spoon by soon,
like the coffee that fills my morning mug.

The Outcast
    (Nathaniel Hawthorne's "Wakefield")

Wakefield steps outside his life as if he were avoiding
a messy puddle, a quick but deliberate move.
His hands warm in his pockets, no luggage
burdens his narrow shoulders.

The streets of London slide open to make a space
but slam shut as he is swallowed by the crowd.
Disguised, escaping from everyone he knows,
Wakefield moves two blocks away.

As impersonal as a controlled experiment,
this Outcast of the Universe wonders what the world
will do without him, certain that he can survive
without society.

His wife shrugs. Sluggish in her distress,
she brushes away his absence as she might
shoo a fly. No lantern lit to welcome as
Wakefield stalks his home and considers returning.

Banishing himself for twenty years, Wakefield
decides, with little thought, to toss the dice and
chance that he would be welcomed back,
accepted again like the Prodigal Son.

Once welcomed, he settles in like an afternoon
rain, book folded in his lap, unfazed by the irony
of stepping back into a life he had shunned, victorious,
as if he had won some ticket in and out.

My Precious One
    (F. Scott Fitzgerald's The Great Gatsby)

Daisy floated in life, bounced upon white sofas,
where sheer curtains framed her pristine rooms.
Her life boasted a darling, precious girl,
stylish hats, famous friends, and a
husband whose wealth ensnared her.

Gatsby followed green lights, in the money
he made, in the go-ahead he followed, in
the green light on Daisy's dock.
Green showed him the way to Daisy,
glittery over rippling waters.

Myrtle lay in the Ash Heaps, riddled
by poverty, discomfort, and a husband
she didn't love. She waited for a passerby
to take her away. And Tom came,
just for a few rides into her heart.

Daisy accidentally ran over Myrtle.
George mistakenly shot Gatsby,
and then himself.
Daisy packed her bags and flew
away with Tom as if nothing happened.

Rich girls don't marry poor boys.
Poor girls don't marry rich men.
Green lights turn red,
and all that glitters is not gold.

Aylmer's Infomercial
    (Nathaniel Hawthorne's "The Birthmark")

My scientific expertise and love for my wife
have merged in the most fascinating way.
Georgianna has a single, small birthmark.
Though she, my Georgianna, sees the mark
as a charm, I see it as the most unfortunate
blemish, a mark of earthly imperfection.

With the aid of my assistant Aminidab,
I shall perform a surgical removal of that faint
but troublesome hand-like print on
fair Georgianna's left cheek. With love
for me and faith in me, she has agreed
to undergo my experiment.

I shall correct what Nature left imperfect
in Her fairest work! Death may occur.
My experiment may result in extreme
repercussions, but I accept the risk
I take for perfection of my Georgianna
and for my craft.

Science has succeeded in removing
the blight, but with that success, Georgianna
has taken Heaven's flight.
She faded as the birthmark does.
My trust in science has kept me from the perfect
future in the present.

All-American
    (Thornton Wilder's Our Town)

George Gibbs was a good boy
who shirked his chores and swung
baseball bats to glory amid adoring crowds.

George Gibbs had big plans.
He would inherit his uncle's farm
 after agricultural school.

But Emily Webb and ice cream sodas
got in his way, stole a base in his
heart and called him out.

The wise Stage Manager married them,
reminded the audience that people
are meant to live two-by-two.

Birth and death met, and Emily
is gone, leaving a grief-stricken
George covering her grave,

and a cynical Simon Stimson accusing
us all of moving in a cloud
of ignorance and self-centeredness.

The dead watch,
and in their wisdom, look at all
the Georges and Emilys
who, like us, don't understand.

Letting Go
    (John Steinbeck's Of Mice and Men)

Lennie squeezed soft things, often too tender
for his beast-big hands. Yearning to hold on
to beauty, his fingers
gripped, his love too tight.

George loved tough, necessary to keep his promise
to Aunt Clara. Taking care of Lennie gave him
purpose, kept him from loneliness but forced
dreadful decisions.

George loved tough enough to put a Ruger
to Lennie's head, sending him early
to their shared dream,
to the rabbits and a life on the fat of the land.

Wanted
>*(Mark Twain's The Adventures of Huckleberry Finn)*

Seek companion, little experience necessary, to escape
on muddy water to a clear path, free of rapscallions,
and the "dag-gum" government.
Prefer someone with innate wisdom, able
to see through the shadows on the river,
able to steer by the shape in his head.
Must be able to role play and avoid
games and taking stock in biblical characters.
Must enjoy star-gazing.

Preferences
(Herman Melville's "Bartleby, the Scrivener")

My name is Bartleby.
My life has been a dead letter,
never belonging to fingers
ripping envelopes for a look inside.
I prefer not to arrive.

My name is Bartleby.
I prefer not to work; I prefer not to eat.
I will not nourish myself with a meal
fed to a world where words are sparse
and human touch faces a brick wall.

My name is Bartleby.
I prefer not to live, to feed selfishly
on the flesh of others.
I prefer to dissolve into the Tombs
and be eaten by things of the quiet earth.

Lucrece and the Modern Woman
(William Shakespeare's "The Rape of Lucrece")

No one held her up for comparison,
to espouse her singular beauty and charm,
the white dove of a suitor's life.
No one extolled her chastity,
no Collatine pride in any knight
or warrior's boast.

Unlike the fair Lucrece, who was a dutiful wife,
she waited not for anyone to surprise her
with a sudden arrival, no husband off to win
her love with a soldier's blade.
She lay asleep in her chamber, answering
no one's rap on the door.

Bitterness and anger fell her door and entered
unannounced. No desire was pilot to this
brutal entrance by a simple acquaintance.
Violence was his sword, a crowbar romanticized.
No son of a king, the rapist had no explanation
or alibi, no "frozen conscience of burning-will."

Both women lost a "dearer thing than life,"
one, her honor, the other her safety.
Lucrece stabbed her breast, fell on the floor
and was covered by her fallen father, he
stained by her blood. The other, walked
into her father's house looking for a way to live.

Collatine's honor overshadowed Lucrece's pain,
leaving no choice but to die, no choice
but to plea for revenge from her sad survivors.
Her peace of mind cut as sharp as Lucrece's dagger,
but left her alive to live with fear in a world
where no one dies for honor.

The Ides of March
    (William Shakespeare's Julius Caesar)

On this day of deception, when Caesar faces his foes,
when Cassius hungers for lean and thinking daggers,
remember Portia, tearing her leg for Brutus,
remember Calpurnia, both bleeding to be heard,
like Cinna the poet, muted, the warning of words.
The power of names, dear Brutus—
His name lends honor to the cause.
His name pushes him forward without pause
his words soothe after Caesar's death.
Brutus flees, runs away from his name,
bearing a dagger, destroyed by fame.

Huck's Heaven
(Mark Twain's The Adventures of Huckleberry Finn)

Must be awful busy past them pearly gates.
Gotta keep someone oiling them things
to work good and shine to welcome the
guests proper.

What with warbling angels and busy harps
it must be kinda noisy 'til you get used to it.
And your eyes tryin' to focus on all that light.

Wonder how the heck you move around
with a crowd huggin' and cryin',
and dogs and cats runnin' to chase rainbows.

Sounds good, but I got a question.
"Answer me this: Am I goin' to eat a banana sandwich with Elvis?"

I been excited about havin' a biscuit
with Abe Lincoln, lunch with Ginger,
my first pony, and a fancy French dinner with Jackie O.

Song says "when we all get to Heaven."
What we goin' to do about first husbands,
second wives, in-laws and sech?

Gotta cousin who worries about that.
Been married four times and can't
decide which one she wants to keep.

Will there be little spaces
where some folks can't go to because
some of the livin' think it just ain't right.

Who is goin' to be first in line for breakfast,
and who decides what is right from wrong?
Or, is there no wrong in Heaven?

That'll be one heck of a place if everybody
is always right and there ain't no need
for Judge Judy or born-again Christians.

There will be so much for us to do
it worries me some that we won't
have time for all that sweet singin.

But Heaven is a place I reckon I'll
check it out, see if it's all that.
Might better make my reservations just in case.

Ain' t never seen Heaven on a map or a TV
commercial, but it sounds like a mighty fine place,
like a Disney World that lasts forever.

Johnston County Arts Council 3rd Place Award

Melinoe's Curse
(Melinoe-the goddess of nightmares)

I dream that my successes
are failures, that skeleton clowns
hide in narrow closets,
wag their bony fingers,
warn that I was good at nothing,
so convincing.

I have dreamed I killed
my mother and father.
I have dreamed
that they killed me, once united,
once each alone.
The twisted gut of family
complicates.
They are dead, but I live to dream,
to fight our battles in the wrap of sleep.

Delights
(Wallace Stevens' "The Emperor of Ice-Cream")

There is delight in creamy, cold ice cream.
The concupiscent curd of Stevens' time
becomes a dripping cone. The melting death,
that life delights with simplicity.
Great rollers of cigars called in for naught,
for nothing matters but the dripping tears.

The daily papers plain and soaked like tears,
soggy, like the cones of melting cream,
treat the falling leaves and snow as naught,
watch with little notice sacred time
and pay no mind to its simplicity
kicked around, stepped over, scattered death.

We pass the horny feet of hateful death,
shed in secrecy the quiet tears,
neglecting to recall simplicity.
We finally lick, before it melts—ice cream
that loses shape so quickly at the time
and dripping there, so sadly turns to naught.

The life of pleasure always comes to naught.
It just provides the sweetness before death.
And when death comes, there is so little time
for grieving. There is only time to see the nothing
that is as delicious as a paper cup-filled ice cream.
Mourners need not make much of the ordinary.

But life's beauty, its treasure hides in the ordinary.
Pretense, conformity breed nothing.
Things are never what they seem, save ice cream,
which when it melts, as it should, there is death.
The realization of death brings unnecessary tears,
for life brings joy one pleasure, one joy, in time.

So many waste and abuse their valuable time,
grab at the illusive, ignore the ordinary.
Greed disappoints, as it flees and brings tears
We understand the everything that seems nothing.
For as we fret and worry about the end, death,
we meet with pleasure the Emperor of ice cream.

Life ends and there is nothing.
The ordinary soothes the finality of death.
Ice cream drips and tears roll down in time.

The Land that Holds Me
    (John Steinbeck's The Grapes of Wrath)

Until the dirt dresses your hands, clothes you, warms you,
sustains you, you cannot know the nakedness of clean
fingers, the loneliness of smooth thumbs, pathetic, empty palms.
My hands are scarred from work, from digging, planting,
weeding, watering. The scars are lines that cover the
inside of my hands. They are maps that trace my life,
my legacy.

Until the dirt is the path you walk, scattered with knobs
of stems and roots, and you find your way through them,
you cannot know how it feels to be headed nowhere.
It is not possible to know the feeling of big machines
replacing the plows my hands guided. The big
machines downing my home, my barns, the things
I built.

My name is Muley Graves. It's not the name my
mama gave me, but it fits me just fine. My
stubborn soul is stone, and I am a part of this land.
My roots are attached to this fertile soil and I grow
with each bloom. I will not clip myself from
that which makes me whole. I am planted
as deep as the wheat and corn I have watched.

My neighbors flee. With misguided plans they
give up who they are for who they hope to be.
I watch them ride through the dust, wipe their
past from their sunken faces.
I will hide from my future. I will forage for food.
I will stay. But my lonely heart runs farther
and deeper than those who rolled away.

In the Harbor
    (Edgar Lee Masters' "George Gray" in Spoon River Anthology)

George has a great big boat to sail.
Chiseling his stone awakens him.
Safe winds and chance his fears repel.

His hunt for meaning always fails.
Fear harbors George and locks him in.
George has a great big boat to sail.

Searching for love reluctance quells.
His hopes for faith he does upend.
Safe winds and chance his fears repel.

George sees no color, his world, pale.
The empty in him sadness sends.
George has a great big boat to sail.

Chickens describe his life so well,
scared and timid he has been.
Safe winds and chance his fears repel.

The dove he wants to no avail.
His destiny on fate depends.
George has a great big boat to sail.
Safe winds and chance his fears repel.

Horizons
    (Zora Neale Hurston's Their Eyes Were Watching God)

He was a "bee to the blossom," this gambling man
who loved to play. Tea Cake knew that life was a trick,
the magic so quick it can't be seen. He invited
Janie to join the game, play her cards, free
her hair to flow in the southern heat.

Tea Cake moved and chased
and cheated to find his way. Janie followed
without thinking. But he had allowed
her own thoughts; she WAS thinking.
She was seeing, she was watching.

Janie called him a "glance from God,"
a wink that made her laugh and love.
Together they were bloom and bite.
He gave her a life and Janie would
never let him take it away.

Tea brought sweetness to her heart
and spirit to her soul. She would never
let him go. Her eyes would watch for
him forever. He showed her a
clear horizon and she moved that way.

Teresa McLamb Blackmon is a North Carolina poet who lives in eastern North Carolina. She is a retired high school English and Journalism teacher. Blackmon received her MA in English from N. C. State University and her MLS from North Carolina Central University. She finished her teaching career as a middle school librarian.

Blackmon began writing in the seventh grade and wrote sporadically through the years. Her first creative writing class piqued her interest. Her professor, Dr. Shelby Stephenson, later the Poet Laureate of North Carolina, encouraged her to "keep writing." In 2021 her first book of poems, *Daddy Said*, was published by Finishing Line Press.

Very active in the literary community in her state, county, and town, Blackmon enjoys taking workshops and offering workshops for the Triangle East Writer's Group and the North Carolina Writer's Network. She also hosts a book club in her hometown, "Southern Exposure Book Club." The focus of the club is on southern literature of all genres.

Blackmon lives on the family farm, a few miles out of town, and enjoys spending time with her four-legged family: a goat, Porter, a miniature donkey, Ruth, a cat, Jazz, and an adorable miniature dachshund, Tia. She is an avid NCSU Wolfpack fan, Democrat, and follower of writer/musician, Kris Kristofferson.